SNAPSHOTS IN HISTORY

FREEDOM RIDES

Campaign for Equality

by Dale Anderson

FREEDOM RIDES

Campaign for Equality

by Dale Anderson

Content Adviser: Stephen Asperheim, Ph.D.,
Assistant Professor of History, Savannah State University

Reading Adviser: Katie Van Sluys, Ph.D.,
School of Education, DePaul University

Compass Point Books ✦ Minneapolis, Minnesota

✣ COMPASS POINT BOOKS

151 Good Counsel Drive
P.O. Box 669
Mankato, MN 56002-0669
877-845-8390
www.capstonepub.com

 This book was manufactured with paper containing at least 10 percent post-consumer waste.

For Compass Point Books
Jennifer VanVoorst, Jaime Martens, Lori Bye, XNR Productions, Inc., Catherine Neitge, Keith Griffin, and Nick Healy

Produced by White-Thomson Publishing Ltd.
For White-Thomson Publishing
Stephen White-Thomson, Susan Crean, Amy Sparks, Tinstar Design Ltd., Stephen Asperheim, Peggy Bresnick Kendler, Brian Fitzgerald, Barbara Bakowski, and Timothy Griffin

Library of Congress Cataloging-in-Publication Data
Anderson, Dale.
  Freedom rides : campaign for equality / by Dale Anderson.
      p. cm. — (Snapshots in history)
  Includes bibliographical references and index.
  ISBN-13: 978-0-7565-3333-5 (library binding)
  ISBN-10: 0-7565-3333-3 (library binding)
1. African Americans—Civil rights—Juvenile literature. 2. Civil rights movements—Southern States—History—20th century—Juvenile literature. 3. Southern States—Race relations—Juvenile literature. I. Title. II. Series.
  E185.61.A544 2007
  323.1196'073075—dc22   2007004916

Printed in the United States of America in Stevens Point, Wisconsin.
012011   006060R

CONTENTS

Attack in Anniston

Chapter

1

Two buses, one owned by the Greyhound bus company and the other by Trailways, moved steadily west across Alabama on May 14, 1961—Mother's Day. The buses were taking the same route they had traveled from Atlanta, Georgia, to Birmingham, Alabama, for years. But there was something unusual about these buses. Each carried several African-American and white civil rights activists. These activists were intent on challenging segregation in the South that forced African-Americans and whites to use separate waiting rooms and eating areas in bus stations.

The civil rights activists had a powerful ally: the U.S. Supreme Court. In December 1960, in the case *Boynton v. Virginia*, the court had declared that segregated waiting rooms violated the U.S. Constitution. That decision inspired the activists

A white official directed an African-American woman to leave the "whites-only" waiting room of a bus station in the South.

to plan a bus trip across several Southern states. The African-Americans in the group planned to enter the whites-only waiting rooms in every bus station they could in order to force state governments to follow the Supreme Court's decision. They called their trip a Freedom Ride.

Although the Freedom Riders had the Supreme Court on their side that day, they needed even greater protection. The activists were riding into grave danger. Members of a racist group called the Ku Klux Klan were determined to defend segregation by stopping the Freedom Riders—

with violence, if necessary. And Klan members in northern Alabama had the cooperation of the local police. Before the Freedom Riders reached Birmingham, a city police official told Klan leaders what they could expect:

> *We're going to allow you fifteen minutes. ... You can beat 'em, bomb 'em, maim 'em, kill 'em. ... There will be absolutely no arrests. You can assure every Klansman in the country that no one will be arrested in Alabama for that fifteen minutes.*

Although the Freedom Riders on the two buses had the same goals, they had different experiences that fateful Mother's Day. The Greyhound bus, carrying seven Freedom Riders, had been the first to leave Atlanta and was the first to reach Alabama. It pulled into the city of Anniston shortly after 1 P.M. An angry crowd of about 50 segregationists immediately rushed toward the bus. Though the door remained closed, preventing them from entering, they did plenty of damage. Some threw rocks or used their fists to smash windows on the bus. Others banged on the sides or slashed the bus's tires.

WHY BUSES MATTERED

In the early 1960s, buses were a major form of transportation. About 370 million trips were taken by bus from one state to another each year. That was more than six times the number of trips people took by air in those years. In the early 2000s, people made about 350 million interstate bus trips, far fewer than the more than 600 million trips that were made by air.

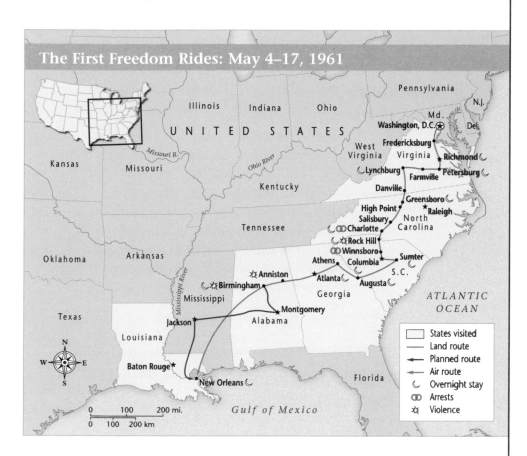

The First Freedom Rides: May 4–17, 1961

The frightening attack continued for about 20 minutes, until police arrived. After telling the segregationists to stop—but making no arrests—the police ordered the bus driver to leave the station. When he pulled out, dozens of vehicles followed. These cars and trucks carried the same angry mob.

A few miles outside town, the bus driver pulled over to change two flat tires. This made the bus an easy target, and the white mob immediately resumed its attack. First they tried to rock the bus to tip it over. When that did not work, they screamed at the riders, demanding they come out. Then someone tossed flaming rags through a

The Freedom Riders began their trip in Washington, D.C., and passed through Virginia, North Carolina, South Carolina, and Georgia before reaching Alabama.

11

broken window. The fire immediately spread to the seats, filling the bus with flames and choking black smoke. Freedom Rider Hank Thomas later described his feelings:

> *I got really scared then. You know, I was thinking—I'm looking out the window there, and people are out there yelling and screaming. They just about broke every window on the bus. ... I really thought that was going to be the end of me. ... [The bus driver] got off, and man, he took off like a rabbit, ... I couldn't very well blame him there. And we were trapped in the bus.*

The Freedom Riders managed to escape the flames by leaving the bus through windows and the door, but there was still danger outside. One attacker bashed Thomas on the head with a baseball bat as soon as he emerged. Others were beaten as well. The Freedom Riders collapsed on the grass, gasping for air and checking their injuries. As the crowd surged toward them, a pair of Alabama highway patrol officers fired shots in the air. That and explosions from the bus convinced the racist mob to scatter.

The injured Freedom Riders were eventually taken to a hospital back in Anniston. When a menacing crowd gathered there, however, hospital officials told the Freedom Riders they had to leave. Their wounds remained untreated. Police ordered the riders to leave town, but first they had to call friends in nearby Birmingham to pick them up. Civil rights activist the Reverend

Fred Shuttlesworth led a convoy of cars from Birmingham to collect the Freedom Riders, who finally left Anniston later that night.

Freedom Riders escaped from the bus and then watched as the Greyhound vehicle burned.

Meanwhile, the seven Freedom Riders on the Trailways bus had no idea what had happened to their fellow activists. That bus had left Atlanta shortly after the Greyhound. Onboard were several Ku Klux Klan members who verbally threatened the Freedom Riders all across Georgia and into Alabama. At the Trailways station in Anniston, the Freedom Riders left the bus, entered the whites-only waiting room, and bought food without a problem—though they were constantly under the hostile eyes of the white people in the station.

Back on the bus, though, trouble began. The driver told two African-American Freedom Riders—Charles Person and Herman Harris—to leave the front seats, which were customarily reserved for whites. When the pair refused, Klan members attacked them, quickly and savagely beating Person and Harris into unconsciousness. Two white Freedom Riders tried to stop the fight, but enraged Klan members turned on them next. They smashed Jim Peck several times in the face and knocked 61-year-old Walter Bergman to the floor of the bus, where one man repeatedly stomped on his chest. Peck and Bergman lost consciousness, too. The Klan members then carried the motionless bodies of Person and Harris to the back seats, and the bus finally left the station.

During the two-hour ride to Birmingham, the four injured Freedom Riders gradually regained consciousness. Their colleagues on the ride tended to their wounds as best they could. When the bus arrived at the Birmingham bus station, the riders remained determined to carry out their mission despite the presence of another angry mob. This was the mob, of course, that had been guaranteed by the city police that they would have 15 minutes to do anything they wanted to the riders.

Peck and Person led the way into the waiting room, but they were quickly attacked and beaten to the ground. So were the other Freedom Riders when they emerged. The mob was so intent on hurting anyone they thought was a Freedom Rider that they even attacked some bystanders.

Finally, after the crowd's promised 15 minutes was up, the police arrived and the crowd melted

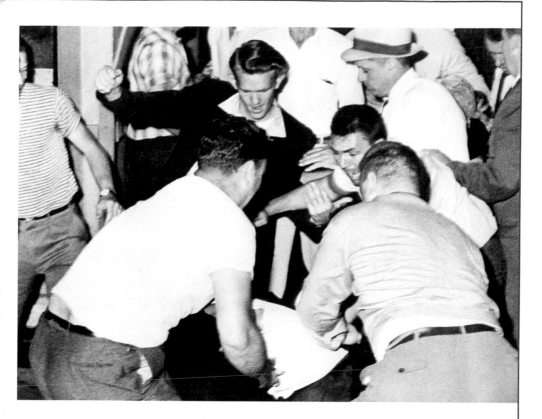

away. The riders found cabs that took them to the safety of Shuttlesworth's church. Peck was taken to a hospital, where he received 53 stitches to close the wounds on his head. But he remained defiant. When reporters asked him what he planned to do, he answered softly but firmly: "The going is getting rougher, but I'll be on that bus tomorrow headed for Montgomery."

Members of the angry mob attacked Freedom Rider Jim Peck (doubled over in foreground) at the Birmingham, Alabama, bus station.

Why were the Freedom Riders willing to put themselves through so much suffering? Why did they submit to this treatment? The answer to those questions lies in the hardship and discrimination that African-Americans faced in the segregated South, and in the principles the civil rights movement developed to end segregation. ◣

The Segregated South

2

The system of segregation in the South began in the decades following the Civil War. That war, fought from 1861 to 1865, had ended African-American slavery and seemed to offer the promise of equal rights for African-Americans. Congress passed several laws aimed at helping the former slaves gain equal rights and a chance for a new life. Congress also passed, and the states approved, three constitutional amendments: The 13th Amendment ended slavery; the 14th Amendment declared that African-Americans were citizens; and the 15th Amendment gave African-American men the right to vote.

Because of deep-seated prejudice against African-Americans, however, many white people in the South resented these changes. Over time, they gained control of the state governments

Signs showing which facilities were meant for African-Americans and which were for whites were common throughout the South.

across the South. Once they did, they passed laws supporting segregation. They set up separate schools for white and black students. They forced the races to use separate hotels, restrooms, restaurants, and other public facilities. The South became a racially divided society.

The Ku Klux Klan arose in the late 1860s, after the Civil War ended, and then declined in importance. Klan membership and violence against African-Americans rose again in the 1920s and 1950s.

Whites made sure that African-Americans could not overturn these laws. Groups such as the Ku Klux Klan used violence or the threat

of violence to convince African-Americans not to vote. Eventually, white-run state and local governments passed laws that took away the voting rights of African-Americans. For instance, they made people pay a tax to vote, which prevented many African-Americans from voting because they were too poor to pay.

The states also put in place literacy tests that required voters to show they could read. African-Americans who could not read were denied a ballot. Whites who could not read were helped by election officials so they could vote anyway. Finally, the states passed "grandfather clauses." These laws said that anyone whose grandfather had not been eligible to vote could not vote. This excluded any African-American whose grandfather had been enslaved. While these laws did not block all African-Americans from voting, black voters in the South were very few.

VIRTUAL SLAVERY

The end of slavery did not bring economic freedom to former slaves. White landowners put in place a system called sharecropping, which prevented African-Americans from making economic gains. Landowners provided seeds and tools to African-American farmers, who grew crops—mainly cotton. At harvest time, the black farmers paid the landowner a share of the crop—as much as two-thirds—and kept the rest. This arrangement kept sharecroppers in debt. Sharecropping was practiced in the South until the 1960s.

African-Americans did not accept this oppressive treatment. Some complained to the federal government—though it did little to protect them. Southern politicians in Washington, D.C., supported segregation. And most politicians from the Northern and Western states had little interest in the problems of Southern blacks. Some blacks challenged segregation laws in the courts. A black citizen named Homer Plessy filed a lawsuit in federal court challenging a Louisiana law requiring segregated railroad cars. In 1896, the U.S. Supreme Court issued its ruling in the case, called *Plessy v. Ferguson*. The majority of the court declared that the state did not violate the Constitution by providing "separate but equal" facilities for whites and African-Americans.

Supreme Court Justice John M. Harlan disagreed. In a dissenting opinion, he explained:

> *In view of the Constitution, in the eye of the law, there is in this country no superior, dominant, ruling class of citizens. ... Our Constitution is color-blind, and neither knows nor tolerates classes among citizens. In respect of civil rights, all citizens are equal before the law. ... The law regards man as man, and takes no account of his surroundings or of his color when his civil rights as guaranteed by the supreme law of the land are involved.*

Despite Harlan's powerful words, the majority decision stood. With *Plessy v. Ferguson*, the court said that segregation was acceptable. Not until the 1940s and 1950s would a different set of justices agree with Harlan and declare segregation unconstitutional.

In the meantime, African-Americans continued to suffer in the segregated South. White leaders claimed that the facilities provided for African-Americans were just as good as those given to whites, but that was rarely true. Schools for whites were in better condition and had newer books. African-American schools were run-down, and the books—if they existed at all—were old and outdated. Whites also controlled the courts, so African-Americans were not allowed to serve on juries.

Most African-American leaders argued that segregated schools were unfair. African-American students usually had substandard books and supplies in their schools.

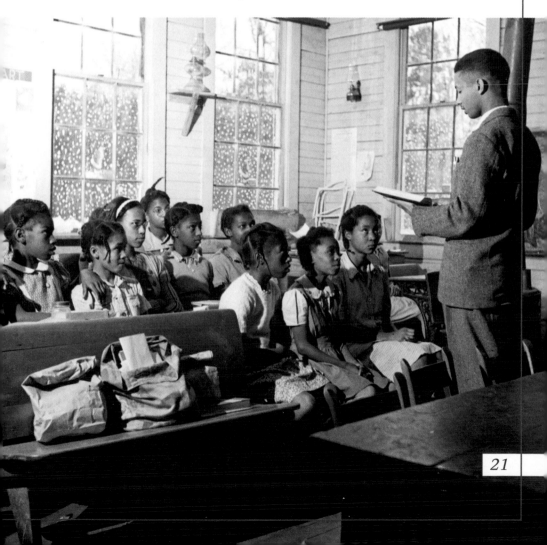

Those who protested risked being taken away in the night by white mobs and beaten or murdered. Each year across the South, dozens of African-Americans were seized and lynched, simply because they tried to resist.

African-Americans developed differing views about how to best respond to segregation. Educator Booker T. Washington believed that they should

Booker T. Washington founded the Tuskegee Institute in Alabama in 1881 and led it until 1915. The Tuskegee Institute trained many African-Americans as teachers and taught crafts and trades to others.

accept limits on their rights for the present and use hard work and discipline to impress white people. Eventually, he believed, white people would see they were wrong and end discrimination. In an 1895 speech in Atlanta, Washington explained:

> *The wisest among my race understand that the agitation of questions of social equality is the extremest folly, and that progress in the enjoyment of all the privileges that will come to us must be the result of severe and constant struggle rather than of artificial forcing. ... It is important and right that all privileges of the law be ours, but it is vastly more important that we be prepared for the exercises of those privileges.*

Historian and social critic W.E.B. Du Bois rejected this approach. He insisted that African-Americans should demand their rights. He said:

> *They [African-Americans] are absolutely certain that the way for a people to gain their reasonable rights is not by voluntarily throwing them away and insisting that they do not want them; that the way for a people to gain respect is not by continuously belittling and ridiculing themselves; ... on the contrary, Negroes must insist continually ... that voting is necessary to proper manhood, that color discrimination is barbarism, and that black boys need education as well as white boys.*

In 1905, Du Bois and others who thought as he did founded a group called the Niagara Movement.

Its goals were to push for full political, civil, and social rights for African-Americans. The group made few gains, however, and many of its members— including Du Bois—joined the National Association for the Advancement of Colored People (NAACP), which had recently been formed.

W.E.B. Du Bois wrote history books that showed the accomplishments of African-Americans and criticized the ways they were treated.

THE FOUNDING OF THE NAACP

In the early 1900s, thousands of African-Americans left the South for the North, hoping to find a better life. As more African-Americans mixed with other ethnicities, racial tensions arose, and sometimes those tensions erupted in race riots that victimized blacks. A particularly violent riot occurred in 1908 in Springfield, Illinois—the home of Abraham Lincoln, who had acted to end slavery during the Civil War. Many reformers—both African-American and white— were shocked by this riot and decided to form a group to try to improve race relations. In 1909, these reformers created the National Association for the Advancement of Colored People (NAACP). The NAACP soon became the foremost organization fighting for equal rights for African-Americans.

The NAACP and other organizations that worked for equal rights for African-Americans did what they could to improve conditions in the South. Still, millions of African-Americans continued to live difficult lives under the harsh policy of segregation, well aware that they were being unfairly and systematically oppressed. ◣

The Growing Civil Rights Movement

Chapter

3

After World War II ended in 1945, African-American groups became increasingly active in their efforts to fight segregation. Thousands of African-Americans had fought in the war, which the U.S. government had called a war to ensure freedom in the world. After putting their lives on the line, African-American men were not willing to accept limits to their own freedom.

Some African-American women bravely challenged these laws as well. A woman named Irene Morgan had been arrested in Virginia for sitting in the whites-only section of a bus that she was taking from Virginia to Maryland. Morgan, with the help of the NAACP Legal Defense and Education Fund, challenged Virginia's segregation law in court. In 1946, the

African-Americans served in segregated military units until 1948, when President Harry Truman ordered that the Army be integrated.

U.S. Supreme Court ruled on the case in *Morgan v. Virginia* that Virginia's law segregating seats on interstate buses violated the U.S. Constitution.

Although the court had spoken, the federal government still made little effort to enforce its ruling. At first some bus companies desegregated their vehicles, but then some of them reversed those orders when pressured by state government officials in the South. Civil rights activists were worried that the landmark Supreme Court decision would result in no changes.

One group—the Congress of Racial Equality (CORE)—decided to take action. In the summer of 1946, Bayard Rustin and George Houser of CORE came up with the idea of a bus trip across Southern states to test the *Morgan* decision. They called the trip the Journey of Reconciliation.

The Journey of Reconciliation included 16 riders—eight African-Americans and eight whites. They traveled for two weeks from Washington, D.C., through Virginia, North Carolina, Tennessee, and Kentucky, and back. At different points,

THE COMMERCE CLAUSE

The federal government was involved in making a decision on the issue of seating on interstate buses because the vehicles were traveling between states. A part of the U.S. Constitution called the commerce clause gives Congress sole power to regulate the flow of commerce between states. Over the years, federal courts decided that paid transportation between states was an example of commerce. As a result, the issue of whether to integrate interstate buses came under the authority of the federal government, rather than state governments.

riders were arrested for breaking segregation laws. When that happened, they paid bail to gain their release and resumed their journey. At some stops, they gave speeches to friendly crowds, hoping to inspire more activism and to spread the word about the power of nonviolent protest.

African-American reporter Ollie Stewart had traveled with the riders to watch what happened. After their return, he described the trip in optimistic terms:

> *The white couple who went to the very back seat and sat between colored passengers, the white Marine who slept while a colored woman sat beside him, the white Southern girl who, when her mother wouldn't take a seat in the rear, exclaimed, "I do not care, I'm tired"—all these people now have an awareness of the problem. ... I heard one man refer to the group [of riders] as pioneers. I think he had something there. They wrote a new page in American history.*

In making the Journey of Reconciliation, CORE challenged segregation through direct action. During the late 1940s and 1950s, the Legal Defense and Education Fund of the NAACP used the courts to challenge segregation laws. The fund filed several lawsuits over the years, each aimed at a particular kind of segregation law.

Starting with *Morgan v. Virginia* in 1946 and ultimately ending with *Brown v. Board of Education* in 1954, the fund repeatedly challenged segregation.

In these important decisions, the U.S. Supreme Court finally rejected the decision earlier justices had made in *Plessy v. Ferguson*. Segregation, the Supreme Court now said, was not allowed.

The chart below shows several major victories the fund won through its efforts.

MAJOR U.S. SUPREME COURT DECISIONS IN THE STRUGGLE FOR CIVIL RIGHTS	
Case	**Decision**
Morgan v. Virginia (1946)	Segregation on interstate buses is unconstitutional.
Patton v. Mississippi (1948)	Excluding African-Americans from juries is unconstitutional.
Shelley v. Kraemer (1948)	Contracts that prohibit the sale of real estate to African-Americans are unconstitutional.
Sweatt v. Painter (1950)	Segregated law schools are unconstitutional.
McLaurin v. Oklahoma (1950)	Segregated state-run graduate schools are unconstitutional.
Henderson v. United States (1950)	Allowing segregated dining cars in an interstate railroad is unconstitutional.
Brown v. Board of Education (1954)	Segregation in public schools is unconstitutional.

As the NAACP challenged the legality of segregation, individuals across the South began to take a stand against oppression. On December 1, 1955, an African-American woman named Rosa Parks was arrested for refusing to give up her seat in the whites-only section of a city bus in Montgomery, Alabama. On December 5, the day of her trial, the city's African-Americans boycotted the city buses in protest.

Rosa Parks' decision not to give up her seat on a city bus was meant to challenge Montgomery's segregation laws.

The boycott worked so well on the day of Parks' trial—so few black people took the buses—that African-Americans in Montgomery decided to continue it. For more than a year, day after day, African-Americans avoided the city buses as part of the Montgomery Bus Boycott. Many walked to work, stores, churches, and schools rather than taking the city buses. Some who had cars turned the vehicles into taxis, ferrying boycotters from place to place. Finally, late in 1956, the Supreme Court ruled in *Gayle v. Browder* that the segregated buses were unconstitutional.

ROSA PARKS (1913–2005)

Rosa Parks was active in her local NAACP chapter when her arrest launched the Montgomery Bus Boycott. A year after the boycott ended, Parks moved to Detroit, Michigan, where she lived the rest of her life, always actively working for civil rights. She received many awards in her life and a singular honor in her death: The U.S. Congress made her the first woman whose body lay in state in the U.S. Capitol. Thousands of people streamed by her coffin to pay their respects to a hero of the civil rights movement.

The Montgomery Bus Boycott also propelled a young minister named Dr. Martin Luther King Jr. into the spotlight. King's eloquent and reassuring speeches helped fuel the determination of thousands of African-Americans to stay off the city buses. He quickly became a major leader of the civil rights movement.

The year after the boycott ended, King and other African-American ministers formed a new group, the Southern Christian Leadership Conference (SCLC).

The group dedicated itself to using nonviolent protest to fight segregation. The principles of nonviolence required activists to challenge unfair laws but do nothing to resist arrest or even physical attack. They had to simply stand still and accept whatever beatings and arrests were delivered. By using these tactics, activists hoped to put pressure on state and local governments across the South by bringing on them the glare of bad publicity and by filling the jails with more prisoners than they could handle. The activists also hoped that by highlighting the way African-Americans' rights were so clearly being violated, they would force the federal government to intervene to help them.

February 1, 1960, marked another step in the struggle for civil rights—one that would help lay the groundwork for the Freedom Rides.

Martin Luther King Jr. rose to national prominence during the Montgomery Bus Boycott.

That day, four young African-American college students sat at the whites-only section of the lunch counter of a Woolworth's store in Greensboro, North Carolina. When they asked to be served, they were turned down. The students refused to leave, however. They remained sitting there until the store closed. The next day, more students joined their sit-in, as their protest was called. By the third day, 80 students were taking part. By the end of the week, other students were carrying out a similar sit-in at the lunch counter of another store in downtown Greensboro.

The sit-in movement spread quickly to other cities. NAACP activists encouraged college students in these cities to stage their own sit-ins. Many students simply took this action on their own, without needing any encouragement from existing civil rights groups.

The sit-ins continued for months, with thousands of African-Americans, many of them college students, taking part. In many cities, the protesters were harassed as whites poured liquids such as ketchup and soft drinks on them as they sat. Many students were arrested for disturbing the peace, even though they were far more orderly than the people who were protesting their actions. And always the students maintained the discipline of nonviolent protest, doing nothing to strike back, no matter what was done to them.

Diane Nash took part in sit-ins in Nashville, Tennessee. She later remembered how determined she and her fellow students were:

> *The police said ... "Everybody's under arrest."*
> *So we all got up and marched to the [police]*
> *wagon. Then they turned and looked around*
> *at the lunch counter again, and the second*
> *wave of students had all taken seats ... then a*
> *third wave. No matter what they did and how*
> *many they arrested, there was still a lunch*
> *counter full of students there.*

In April, 2,500 students marched to Nashville's city hall. Nash asked Mayor Ben West point-blank whether he thought it was morally right to have segregated lunch counters. West said no, and soon merchants in that city stopped segregating.

After the initial sit-in in Greensboro, North Carolina, many other African-American college students joined the effort.

Eventually, stores in other cities did the same. Later in 1961, Woolworth's and other chain stores announced that they would integrate their lunch counters. Once again, mass protests had created a major victory for civil rights.

The sit-ins also spawned a new organization. Ella Baker, a leading figure in the SCLC, saw the spirit of the college students in the sit-in movement and decided it was time to harness this commitment. Baker organized a meeting in the spring of 1960 in Raleigh, North Carolina, and invited students from across the South who were active in the sit-ins.

At the three-day meeting, the students embraced the idea of nonviolent protest, but they also declared their desire not to join the SCLC. They wanted their own organization. Baker encouraged them, and they formed a new group, the Student Nonviolent Coordinating Committee (SNCC).

Many of the Nashville protesters played important roles in forming SNCC. One of them, James Lawson, inspired the other students with his words about nonviolence:

> *Through nonviolence, courage displaces fear; love transforms hate. Acceptance dissipates [dissolves] prejudice; hope ends despair. Peace dominates war; faith reconciles doubt. Mutual regard cancels enmity [hate]. Justice for all overthrows injustice. The redemptive community supersedes systems of gross social immorality.*

SNCC BREAKS THROUGH

After its creation in 1960, the Student Nonviolent Coordinating Committee (SNCC) quickly moved onto the national political scene. That year was a presidential election year, and the Democratic and Republican parties held their national conventions that summer to choose presidential candidates. Members of SNCC asked for—and were granted—the opportunity to address the committees writing the two parties' platforms, or statements of principles and goals. In their presentation, SNCC members urged both parties to move quickly to bring equal rights to African-Americans.

From the start, though, members of SNCC were divided on which goals to pursue. Some SNCC members wanted to continue actions like sit-ins to end segregation. Others believed that the movement should focus on efforts to register as many African-Americans as possible in the South to vote. Only by voting in strength, they felt, could African-Americans effectively gain civil rights. Leaders of SNCC were unwilling to push local student groups to take specific actions. They believed that local groups should develop their own plans and that the national organization should simply coordinate them and encourage them.

Divided and unwilling to push for national goals, SNCC did not take strong actions through the rest of 1960 and into early 1961. In fact, it wasn't until the Freedom Rides later in 1961 that members of SNCC found an action they wanted to take. ◾

The First Wave of Rides

The 1947 Journey of Reconciliation tested the Supreme Court's decision in *Morgan v. Virginia*. In 1961, civil rights activists once again set out to use interstate bus travel as a way to end segregation. This effort—the Freedom Rides— was also inspired by a 1960 U.S. Supreme Court decision, *Boynton v. Virginia*. In this decision, the court ruled that having segregated facilities in the waiting rooms of bus stations that served interstate buses was unconstitutional.

Early in 1961, soon after the court issued the ruling, James Farmer became director of CORE. On his first day on the job, he and his staff discussed how to respond to the *Boynton* decision. Two staffers had a suggestion—to repeat the 1947 Journey of Reconciliation, this time calling the trip a Freedom Ride.

African-Americans who had lived in the North were shocked when they encountered segregation at bus terminals and other public facilities in the South.

COLORED
WAITING ROOM
INTRASTATE PASSENGERS →

← PULLMAN PASSENGERS
CHECK WITH PULLMAN
CONDUCTOR AT RECEIVING
TABLE BEFORE GOING TO
TRAINS 4-11-&-36
CARS A-4-54-47-&S-58

Farmer spent the next weeks recruiting African-Americans and whites to take part in the rides and training them in the principles of nonviolence. Some were members of CORE; some were people who were active in civil rights through other organizations or who were ready to join the movement. At 18, Charles Person was the youngest rider, and 61-year-old Walter Bergman was the oldest.

JAMES FARMER

James Farmer graduated from Howard University in Washington, D.C., in 1941 and the next year helped found the Congress of Racial Equality (CORE). Deeply committed to nonviolence, he wrote those principles into CORE's charter. Farmer continued working for civil rights until his death in 1999. In 1998, President Bill Clinton awarded him a Presidential Medal of Freedom.

The Freedom Riders included some people who had spent their entire lives in the South and others who had lived only in the North. Several were college students. Three—Bergman's wife, Frances, Genevieve Hughes, and Mae Frances Moultrie—were women. Only Jim Peck had taken the Journey of Reconciliation.

The plan called for a trip from Washington, D.C., to New Orleans, Louisiana. On this trip, the Freedom Riders would cross the Deep South, the states from South Carolina to Louisiana. The goal was to reach New Orleans in time for the anniversary of the U.S. Supreme Court's decision in *Brown v. Board of Education*. Civil rights activists were planning an important rally to mark that historic day. Travel through the Deep South was bold—and dangerous—

Before beginning the Freedom Rides, James Farmer sent a CORE worker on a bus trip to the South to see where the riders might expect to find trouble.

because racial prejudice was stronger in these states than in Virginia, North Carolina, and Tennessee. Still, the CORE activists believed that to make their point, they had to ensure that the law applied even in the Deep South.

They also took precautions. Before the riders set out, Farmer sent information about their plans to President John F. Kennedy, Attorney General Robert Kennedy (the president's brother), Director of the Federal Bureau of Investigation J. Edgar Hoover, and the presidents of the two bus companies. None of them responded.

41

The trip began on May 4, 1961. At first, there were 12 riders. Farmer, who was one of the 12, split them into two groups: One would take a Greyhound bus; the other would ride a Trailways bus. On each bus, at least one African-American rider would sit in the traditional whites-only section. At least one pair of Caucasian and African-American riders would sit next to each other, breaking another Southern custom. Two other riders could sit anywhere. At least one African-American rider, however, had to sit in the back of the bus. That person, Farmer hoped, would not be arrested and could call CORE headquarters to report on any trouble that developed.

The Freedom Rides were relatively uneventful through both Virginia and North Carolina. On May 9, the riders reached Rock Hill, South Carolina,

During their first few days on the road, the Freedom Riders did not face the angry crowds that would await them later in their trip.

42

and met the first violence. A gang of white men punched two riders—John Lewis, an African-American, and Al Bigelow, a Caucasian—several times before the police scattered the attackers.

That night, as the riders rested, Lewis received surprising news. He had been offered a chance at a grant of money to spend two years abroad studying nonviolence. In order to receive the money, though, he had to leave immediately for an interview in Philadelphia. Reluctantly, Lewis left, hoping to return in a few days.

JOHN LEWIS

In 1961, John Lewis was a 21-year-old student at a Baptist seminary in Nashville, Tennessee. Born in rural Alabama, Lewis was inspired to enter the civil rights movement by hearing speeches on the radio from Martin Luther King Jr. Lewis helped form the Student Nonviolent Coordinating Committee (SNCC) and took part in its first demonstrations. Lewis was SNCC's chairman from 1963 to 1966, and he participated in many of the civil rights movement's major actions in that period. He was elected to Congress from Georgia in 1986.

Two days later, the riders lost another member when Benjamin Cox, a minister, left to return to his church so he could conduct Sunday services. He, too, expected to rejoin the group. Farmer called for four new riders to join them.

Nothing serious occurred through the rest of South Carolina or on the road to Atlanta, Georgia. There, on the night of May 13, the riders had dinner with Martin Luther King Jr. He offered them words of encouragement, but at the end of the meal, he pulled aside Simeon Booker, a journalist covering the Freedom Rides. "You will never make it through Alabama," King warned.

The riders lost a key member that night. Farmer received a phone call telling him that his father had died. Torn, Farmer finally decided he had to leave the ride to be with his mother. Later he recalled his mixed feelings that night:

> *Like everyone else, I was afraid of what lay in store for us in Alabama, and now that I was to be spared participation in it, I was relieved, which embarrassed me to tears.*

The day after Farmer left, the Freedom Rides set out from Atlanta, Georgia, for Birmingham, Alabama. Events showed that King's prediction was correct. The riders on one bus were brutally attacked outside the city of Anniston, Alabama, by members of an angry mob of whites. These riders managed to reach Birmingham, but only because they were carried there in the cars of civil rights activists who came to rescue them. The second group of riders passed through Anniston without incident, but

A brutal attack occurred on the Greyhound bus between Atlanta, Georgia, and Birmingham, Alabama.

45

they were attacked at the bus station in Birmingham. That night, the riders from both buses gathered in Birmingham in the homes of people committed to helping them.

On May 15, the Monday after those brutal attacks, the riders discussed what to do next. Local and national news reports described the battering of the riders and criticized the police for being nowhere in sight. Attorney General Robert Kennedy then promised to work out a police escort for the bus through the rest of Alabama. With this good news, the riders left for the bus station in Birmingham to continue their journey.

Obstacles appeared, though, as they prepared to continue the Freedom Rides. Alabama Governor John Patterson issued a statement calling the Freedom Riders rabble-rousers and saying he could not protect them from white Alabamans. The Greyhound company said it could not find anyone to drive a bus with the riders in it. All that Monday, the riders ended up huddled together in the bus station, surrounded by a mob of angry whites being held off by the city police.

Late in the afternoon, the riders decided to abandon the buses. They felt frustrated by being unable to carry out their plan, but they wanted to reach New Orleans in time for the activities marking the anniversary of the *Brown* decision. As they were shuttled to the airport by African-American drivers, the mob raced after them. Soon the riders were under siege again.

Late that night, John Siegenthaler, an aide to Attorney General Kennedy, worked out an arrangement that would allow the riders to leave the city in secret. Just before midnight, the Freedom Riders left Birmingham for New Orleans with Siegenthaler on the plane as well. It seemed the Freedom Ride was over.

Alabama Governor John Patterson refused to protect the Freedom Riders.

47

The Second Wave: To Montgomery

Chapter

5

The first wave of Freedom Rides was, indeed, over. But more were to come, and they began almost immediately. SNCC activists in Nashville, Tennessee, launched the second wave of Freedom Rides. These activists had staged the Nashville sit-in the year before and had also recently enjoyed success integrating the city's movie theaters. They had followed the first wave of Freedom Rides closely. News of the violence in Alabama had shocked them, and they immediately began discussing how to respond. When they heard that the CORE Freedom Riders had decided not to continue, SNCC decided to replace them.

Diane Nash, a leader of the Nashville group, raised enough money to buy 10 bus tickets. She called the Reverend Fred Shuttlesworth in

Birmingham to say that the students were coming. He warned her that the other Freedom Riders had almost been killed. Nash replied firmly:

That's exactly why the ride must not be stopped. If they stop us with violence, the movement is dead. We're coming. We just want to know if you can meet us.

Another Nashville leader, James Bevel, selected the 10 riders. John Lewis had returned from his Philadelphia interview by this time, and he was the

The Reverend Fred Shuttlesworth was concerned for the safety of the Nashville Freedom Riders.

DIANE NASH

Diane Nash was born in 1938 to a middle-class African-American family. Growing up in Chicago, she had little exposure to the extreme racism suffered by blacks in the South. An excellent student, she went to Howard University in Washington, D.C., and then to Fisk University in Nashville. There she first encountered the limits that racism placed on blacks' lives, and she was outraged. Determined to do something, she began to take part in workshops on nonviolent protest. Highly respected by the other students who formed SNCC, Nash became an early leader of the group.

first. Bevel chose seven other African-Americans— five males and two females—along with a white man and woman. Late on Tuesday, May 16, the second wave of riders went home to pack. Knowing the danger they faced, some wrote wills.

The Freedom Riders set out from Nashville on May 17 and reached Birmingham by midday. City police met the bus at the city limits. They quickly arrested riders James Zwerg, a Caucasian, and Paul Brooks, an African-American, for breaking segregation laws by sitting together. Then the police escorted the bus to the station. Once there, they checked the tickets of all the passengers onboard. The seven holding tickets from Nashville to New Orleans via Birmingham were suspected of being Freedom Riders and were held on the bus. Other passengers were allowed to leave.

Those who departed included one rider who had bought her ticket in a different town. She quickly called Nash and told her about what had taken place. Nash, in turn, called the Justice Department in Washington, D.C., to ask why the Freedom Riders were being held. Burke Marshall, an official in the Justice Department, promised to look into the matter.

After being held on the bus for an hour, the riders were allowed to leave the bus. They walked through a jeering crowd—restrained by police officers—into the station. They insisted on taking the next bus to Montgomery. When they moved to get on that bus, T. Eugene "Bull" Connor, who headed Birmingham's police, ordered them arrested.

T. Eugene "Bull" Connor staunchly supported segregation and used his power— and brute force—to enforce segregation laws in Birmingham.

The situation had reached a stalemate. Governor Patterson had refused to protect the Freedom Riders, and the riders refused to return to Nashville. Meanwhile, Attorney General Robert Kennedy and his advisers met with President John F. Kennedy to decide what to do. They hoped to force Patterson to protect the riders, but the federal officials held out little hope that he would agree to do so.

In the meantime, the federal government made plans to gather a force of U.S. marshals and other federal law enforcement officers. As a last resort, they would use these officers to protect the riders, but they did not wish to do so unless it was absolutely necessary, because that would damage their standing among Southern white voters.

That night, Bull Connor revealed his own solution to the problem of the Freedom Riders. He packed seven of the 10 riders into police cars and drove them north, to Alabama's border with Tennessee. One female rider had been released earlier to her father, who had flown down to Birmingham to collect her. Zwerg and Brooks had been released separately and were not with the seven other riders. The Birmingham police left the riders on the Tennessee side of the border and told them to go back to Nashville.

Connor had not reckoned with the determination of the students, though. Once the riders had been arrested, Nash had sent 11 more students from Nashville to Birmingham to continue the Freedom

Rides. And the seven who had been dropped in Tennessee resolved to return to Alabama as well. The next day, a driver sent by Nash carried them back to Birmingham.

On Friday, May 19, Zwerg, Brooks, and the other 18 riders walked into the bus station to take a bus to Montgomery. By this time, approximately 3,000 people milled in and around the station. They harassed the riders as they waited for their next bus—spilling drinks on them or stepping on their feet. Officials with the Greyhound bus company announced that it had no driver for them. The riders simply waited, singing religious songs and preaching.

"BULL" CONNOR'S POWER

T. Eugene "Bull" Connor was the commissioner of public safety in Birmingham, Alabama, from 1937 to 1954 and from 1958 to 1963. In that post, he led the city's police and fire departments. Connor used police force and cooperation with the Ku Klux Klan to prevent African-American activists from enjoying any success in ending segregation in Birmingham. In 1963, Connor ordered police and firefighters to use fierce dogs and fire hoses to stop a civil rights march that included children. His heavy-handed action backfired, though, by producing sympathy for the civil rights movement.

Robert Kennedy and Alabama officials negotiated through the night and the next day to resolve the crisis. Finally, Governor Patterson agreed to provide security to the Freedom Riders on the highway. Then a new problem arose. Just before the bus was to leave on Saturday morning, the driver told the riders he would not take the wheel: "I don't have but one life to give. And I don't intend to give it to CORE or the NAACP. And that's all I have to say."

Two hours later, company officials convinced the driver to make the trip. The bus rolled out of the station, accompanied by Birmingham city police up to the city limits. There it was met by cars full of state troopers. Also along for the ride were U.S. marshals and cars full of reporters. The whole convoy roared down the highway at almost 90 miles (144 kilometers) per hour. The vehicles moved so fast under orders of Alabama officials, who wanted to get the bus out of their state as quickly as possible.

Just before the bus arrived in Montgomery, though, city police who had been at the station began to disappear. As the Freedom Riders got off the bus, they were swarmed by a group of reporters looking for comments. Then a new force arrived—a large mob of angry whites carrying baseball bats, lead pipes, and broken bottles. They brushed the reporters aside and attacked.

The Freedom Riders tried to escape. Some jumped into nearby taxicabs, though they were prevented from getting away when the mob blocked the exits. Lewis tried to lead some riders to an African-American church, but that group was trapped and brutally beaten. Jim Zwerg was smashed in the face with a suitcase and then repeatedly punched. Lewis was hit in the face with a wooden crate.

Justice Department official John Siegenthaler, who had returned from taking the first wave of Freedom Riders to New Orleans, was on the scene. He tried to rescue two of the riders, but someone in the mob smashed his head with a pipe, knocking him unconscious. The rampaging attackers also assaulted reporters and photographers who were recording the scene.

Ten minutes later, the city police returned and stopped the beatings. They were followed by the Alabama attorney general, who read a court order from a state judge that told the riders they

The blood-spattered clothing of John Lewis (left) and Jim Zwerg showed the ferocity of the crowd that had attacked them and other Freedom Riders in Birmingham.

55

could not continue their Freedom Ride through Alabama. The riders, bleeding and barely conscious, found it difficult to understand what was being said. They waited a long time to get transportation to hospitals.

Some of the riders did manage to escape. They phoned Diane Nash for instructions. She told

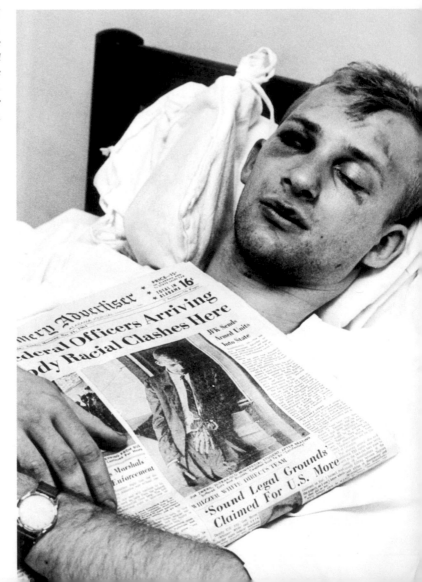

As he lay in a hospital bed on May 21, 1961, Jim Zwerg read about the beating he had suffered a day earlier outside the Montgomery bus station. He remained in the hospital for five days.

them all to gather at the house of S.S. Seay, a local minister. All that night, the riders trickled in, glad to see that their colleagues had survived. Despite the horrors of the day, they remained ready to continue. Even those still in the hospital were grimly determined. As Jim Zwerg told reporters:

> *These beatings cannot deter us from our purpose. We are not martyrs or publicity-seekers. We want only equality and justice, and we will get it. We will continue our journey one way or another. We are prepared to die.* ◣

After Montgomery

Chapter

6

After the attacks on the Freedom Riders in Montgomery, Attorney General Robert Kennedy no longer felt he could count on Alabama authorities to cooperate. He decided to send in federal law enforcement personnel.

Meanwhile, the situation had grown even more dangerous. Martin Luther King Jr. decided to come to Montgomery to speak at a rally the night of May 21, 1961. King, Shuttlesworth, and others would use the rally to express their support for the Nashville students. Knowing the danger that King faced in entering Montgomery, Kennedy ordered federal marshals to meet his plane and protect him.

On the night of May 21, about 1,500 African-Americans gathered in Montgomery's First

The Freedom Riders were invited to a rally at Montgomery's First Baptist Church. The large crowd applauded heartily when the riders were introduced.

Baptist Church to hear King and others speak. Several federal marshals stood outside the church, hoping to maintain order. In a park across the street, a crowd of whites gathered. By nightfall, they were in a foul mood.

James Farmer, his father now buried, had traveled to Montgomery, too. But before he left, he told his staff to gather a new set of Freedom Riders. He wanted CORE to lead the way once again. Miraculously, the Reverend Shuttlesworth managed to bring Farmer safely through the crowd after picking him up at the airport.

Meanwhile, Robert Kennedy was constantly on the phone with aides in Alabama. When he was told that the mob had overturned and ignited a car and was throwing rocks at the church, he ordered a larger force of U.S. marshals to the church. When they arrived, they

RULES OF JURISDICTION

Different leaders had control over different groups meant to enforce order during the Freedom Rides. Local officials controlled the police in cities such as Birmingham and Montgomery. Each police force had power only within its city limits. State governors, such as Alabama's John Patterson, controlled the state police. They were also in charge of troops of the National Guard, an emergency military force that is organized by states. In some crises during the civil rights movement, the president of the United States moved to place the National Guard under federal control. Once that action was taken, the troops had to obey the president and not their state's governor. Law enforcement officers who worked for the federal government were under the control of the president as well. They included people such as U.S. marshals and agents of the Federal Bureau of Investigation.

fired tear gas at the crowd of angry whites, but when it began to clear, some members of the mob surged forward again. They threw rocks through the windows of the church and fired gunshots into the homes of African-Americans living on the street. The situation had become a crisis.

Just then, National Guard troops arrived. More numerous and better armed than the marshals, they took control. They held back the mob—but they also prevented the tired and fearful African-Americans inside the church from leaving, saying they could not protect them as they traveled to their own homes. All night long, the congregation huddled in the church. Finally, federal officials

African-Americans in the doorway of the First Baptist Church watched as National Guard troops arrived to restore order in the area around the church.

convinced the National Guard commander to let the people go. At 4:30 A.M., National Guard trucks began ferrying people back to their homes.

For the next two days, Nash, Bevel, and the SNCC riders discussed their next steps. Some tried to convince King to join them, but he declined. Several riders felt less impressed with King as a result. Twelve riders debated another issue. They were students at a Tennessee state college, and the governor of Tennessee had threatened to have them expelled if they continued the trip. Eleven of them reluctantly decided to return to Nashville. At the same time, more and more volunteers arrived in Montgomery to join the Freedom Rides.

Meanwhile, Robert Kennedy and his aides discussed with officials in Alabama and Mississippi—the riders' next destination—how to protect the activists. They worked out a plan that would give the Freedom Riders an escort from federal and state officials along the route from Montgomery, Alabama, to Jackson, Mississippi. Once they reached Jackson, though, the riders would be arrested. Kennedy's agreement with this part of the plan caused bad feelings among many civil rights activists once they learned of it.

On May 24, the Freedom Riders set out. National Guardsmen escorted them to the bus station, where 500 armed troops stood by. Twelve riders got on a Trailways bus along with several reporters and a handful of National Guard troops. There were no regular passengers. The bus left the station and sped down the road, accompanied by a caravan of National Guard vehicles.

The Freedom Riders were told there would be no stops—the bus would simply keep going until it reached the Mississippi border. They bristled, but they had no choice. At the Mississippi border, they were handed over to the Mississippi National Guard and once again sped along their way at 70 miles (112 km) per hour.

Attorney General Robert F. Kennedy admired the moral courage of the Freedom Riders but was also angered by their determination to continue.

As the Trailways bus sped west, a second group of 15 riders turned up at the Montgomery Greyhound station ready to travel, to the surprise of state and federal authorities. They were hastily boarded onto a bus as the National Guard troops continued to hold back the crowd. This group included John Lewis and other veterans of the early part of the second wave. It also included James Farmer.

Freedom Riders prepared to board the bus in Montgomery that would take them to Mississippi. This time they were surrounded not by an angry mob but by a crowd of journalists and National Guard troops sent to protect them.

The journey of the second bus repeated that of the first, though officials had to scramble to find the law enforcement and National Guard troops to provide the needed protection. At the Mississippi border, an Alabama state police official whispered something to one of the reporters on the bus, who talked to the others. They all left. Just before they got off, the reporter told Farmer that

there were reports the bus would be ambushed as it moved through Mississippi. The riders faced their growing alarm by singing freedom songs.

As the second bus sped west, the first pulled into the bus station in Jackson, Mississippi, where police were waiting. The 12 riders entered the whites-only waiting room and began to walk to the restroom reserved for whites. Told to leave by a police captain, they refused. They were promptly arrested, charged with crimes such as disobeying a police officer and disturbing the peace.

A few hours later, the second bus brought the second set of riders into Jackson. City police officers formed two lines to make a corridor the riders could walk through into the whites-only waiting room at the bus station. As soon as they stepped inside, they, too, were arrested.

Then came another surprise to government officials. A group of white clergymen and African-Americans from the North arrived in Montgomery, determined to make their own Freedom Ride. This group included the chaplain of Yale University,

Police officers searched a Freedom Rider during their arrests. The riders, following their philosophy of nonviolent protest, did nothing to resist their arrests, but the activists were shocked that the federal government had allowed them to be charged.

The Reverend Ralph Abernathy (right) joined the Freedom Rides and was later arrested in Montgomery.

a Yale professor, and two professors from Wesleyan University in Connecticut. They were pelted with rocks by the crowd, still gathered at the station, until they could be taken away to the house of the Reverend Ralph Abernathy, an associate of King's.

BAD TIMING FOR THE PRESIDENT

After the second group of riders had appeared at the Greyhound station in Birmingham, Attorney General Robert Kennedy had issued an angry statement. While he did not want the riders to be hurt, he complained that they were undermining the position of his brother, the president, just before an important summit meeting with the leader of the Soviet Union, Nikita Khrushchev. The statement said: "Whatever we do in the United States at this time which brings or causes discredit on our country can be harmful to his mission." Reporters asked Abernathy for his thoughts on Kennedy's statement. Abernathy had no sympathy: "Well, doesn't the attorney general know we've been embarrassed all our lives?"

The appearance of the third group outraged Robert Kennedy. He issued a statement calling for a cooling-off period—a temporary end to the Freedom Rides. The group from the North did not comply. The next day—May 25—the seven Northerners went to the bus station in Montgomery to board a bus for Mississippi. They were promptly arrested, along with Abernathy, Shuttlesworth, and two others who were with them.

But the attorney general would have to face one more surprise. He hoped the Freedom Riders would post bail, go home, and end what had become, to him, a nightmare of bad publicity. Once again, the Freedom Riders refused to do the easy thing. They decided to remain in the Jackson jail and await their trial. ◣

The Later Rides

Members of the Kennedy administration perhaps thought their difficulties with the Freedom Riders were over, but they were wrong. King and representatives of CORE and SNCC had been discussing keeping up the pressure. On May 26, 1961, the day after the third busload of riders left Montgomery, the civil right leaders announced that they had formed a new group—the Freedom Ride Coordinating Committee. Its task was to continue the Freedom Rides throughout the summer. The committee did not lack volunteers; hundreds of people were calling CORE and SNCC, asking to become Freedom Riders.

The decision to continue the Freedom Rides was not a popular one. *The New York Times* issued an editorial criticizing the idea, and a public

Four civil rights leaders—(from left) James Farmer, Ralph Abernathy, Martin Luther King Jr., and John Lewis—announced to the press their determination to continue the Freedom Rides throughout the summer of 1961.

THE PRESIDENT SPEAKS

The night of May 25, 1961, President John F. Kennedy addressed Congress in a special State of the Union address. He said nothing about the Freedom Rides but instead discussed the nation's Cold War struggle with the Soviet Union. As part of that struggle, he pledged to strengthen the country's new space program and land an American on the moon before the decade ended. Many people involved in the civil rights struggle were unimpressed. Rabbi Edward E. Klein commented, "It seems strange to discuss trips to the moon when it is impossible for white and colored Americans to travel together on a bus and use the same facilities in 'the land of the free and the home of the brave.'"

opinion poll showed that more than 60 percent of Americans did not approve of the Freedom Rides. But the civil rights activists continued with their mission.

For the next several months, more than 400 people took part in dozens of Freedom Rides. Slightly more than half the riders were African-Americans, and about three-quarters were male.

Most Freedom Riders traveled on buses, but some took trains, challenging segregation in train stations. Some trips crossed only one state line, and others traveled across several states. From May through July, most Freedom Riders traveled to Jackson, Mississippi, carrying out the plan that activists developed—filling Mississippi jails and prisons with nonviolent protesters. They succeeded, and more than 320 riders were arrested in Jackson that spring and summer.

When he was arrested, rider William Mahoney had a calm conversation with a Jackson policeman that revealed the gulf of attitudes between the riders and many white Southerners. As Mahoney later recounted:

> *While being interrogated I asked the detective if he knew that legally and by the moral standards America professes to the world we had a right to act as we did and that his actions were helping to tear down any respect that the world might have had for our country. He said that this might be so but that the South had certain traditions which must be respected.*

The Freedom Rides of May 1961 generated a great deal of news coverage. As the rides continued, however, the stories dwindled. That did not lessen the determination of the riders.

Southern police officers and guards were even more puzzled by the participation of whites in the Freedom Rides. One Mississippi guard marveled at their behavior, saying:

> *I can't understand them white boys up there. They can go anywhere they wanna go, they're white. What they come down here for?*

A group of white riders left New York City for Washington, D.C., to pressure the Kennedy administration to act more strongly to promote civil rights.

In mid-June, new cities were targeted on the Freedom Rides. On June 13, two large groups set out from Washington, D.C., for a trip of several days to two cities in Florida. In mid-July, other Freedom Rides traveled to New Orleans, Louisiana, and Little Rock, Arkansas.

Meanwhile, the riders arrested on May 24 spent several weeks in prison. They lived in miserable conditions. Each female prisoner had her own cell, which was 13 feet by 15 feet (4 meters by 4.5 meters). Males, however, were packed three to a cell, and each cell was less than half the size of a woman's cell. The food was awful. Breakfast biscuits were so hard that one prisoner carved them into shapes. When Farmer complained, the warden dismissed him. "We want you to stay in there and rot," he said. "We got to feed you because the law says we gotta feed you." The imprisoned riders were subjected to petty annoyances, like wrong-sized underwear and having their mattresses taken away. Still, they persevered.

By riding the buses and integrating the bus stations, the riders were exercising their constitutional rights. All the arrests were made on fabricated charges such as disturbing the peace. Still, the Kennedy administration was willing to allow the riders to be arrested rather than risk the severe physical abuse and violence that had marred the first two waves of Freedom Rides.

At the same time, the administration tried two new approaches to defuse the situation. On May 29, the Monday after the arrests of the second wave of riders, Robert Kennedy met with his staff to discuss the situation. They decided to adopt a strategy that King had suggested earlier: They asked the Interstate Commerce Commission (ICC) to issue a ruling on segregated bus stations. Although the Supreme Court had declared segregated bus stations unconstitutional, that ruling would have little effect if not enforced. The ICC—the federal agency that regulated interstate bus travel—was the arm of the federal government with the power to enforce the court's ruling.

The second part of the plan involved campaigning with civil rights groups for a change in strategy. For a long time, the Kennedy administration had been urging civil rights groups to stop massive actions of civil disobedience like the Freedom Rides. Instead, federal officials said, civil rights activists should work to register African-American voters in the South. The officials said that the more African-Americans who registered to vote, and voted, the sooner they could get segregationist politicians out of office in the South.

THE SINGER-ACTIVIST

Robert Kennedy recruited a celebrity to help him persuade civil rights leaders to support the voter registration effort. The popular folk singer Harry Belafonte had a deep commitment to the civil rights movement. He was also friendly with Kennedy. In June 1961, Kennedy persuaded Belafonte to meet with SNCC leaders to push the voter registration idea. Belafonte not only urged the point but offered SNCC $10,000 to get the work started.

Attorney General Kennedy met with members of the Freedom Ride Coordinating Committee in mid-June to persuade them to follow this approach. Civil rights leaders finally agreed to this strategy, convinced in part because three foundations offered money to fund the effort.

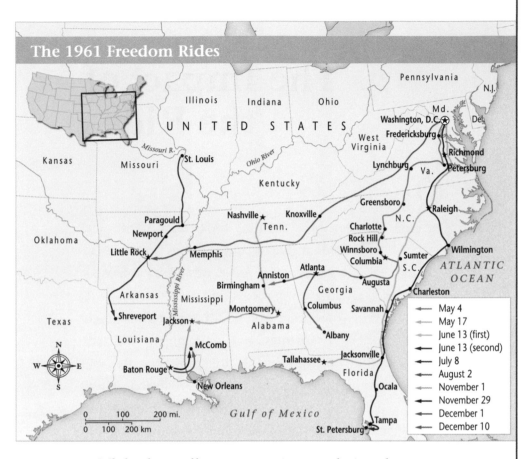

The 1961 Freedom Rides

Pennsylvania
N.J.

Illinois   Indiana   Ohio

UNITED STATES

Md.
Washington, D.C.

Del.

West   Fredericksburg
Virginia

Richmond

Kansas   Missouri R.   St. Louis   Lynchburg   Richmond
Missouri   St. Louis   Ohio River   Va.   Petersburg

Kentucky

Greensboro
Nashville   Knoxville   Raleigh
N.C.
Paragould   Tenn.   Charlotte
Newport   Rock Hill   Wilmington
Little Rock   Memphis   Winnsboro   Sumter
Columbia   S.C.   ATLANTIC
Atlanta   OCEAN
Anniston   Augusta
Birmingham   Georgia   Charleston
Arkansas   Mississippi
Columbus   Savannah
Shreveport   Jackson   Montgomery
Texas   Alabama
Louisiana   Albany
McComb
Tallahassee   Jacksonville
Baton Rouge   Florida
New Orleans   Ocala

Oklahoma

Kansas

Gulf of Mexico

0   100   200 mi.
0   100   200 km

Tampa
St. Petersburg

←	May 4
←	May 17
←	June 13 (first)
←	June 13 (second)
←	July 8
←	August 2
←	November 1
←	November 29
←	December 1
←	December 10

While these efforts were going on during the summer and fall of 1961, the Freedom Rides continued. Finally, the ICC issued its decision on September 23. It declared that segregated waiting rooms were illegal—a decision, of course, that the Supreme Court had made the previous December. More important, the ICC detailed the punishments that would result from a violation of its rules. It specified fines that would have to be paid by all parties—including bus companies—that used segregated facilities. The new rules would take effect on November 1, 1961.

From May through December 1961, Freedom Riders traveled through much of the southern United States.

77

The Impact of the Rides

Chapter

8

After the ICC ruling took effect, CORE sent Freedom Riders out on bus journeys to make sure that the order was being followed. Nearly all waiting rooms had been desegregated. When they were not, CORE reported the facts to bus companies and government officials, who worked to fix the situation. Soon the sole trouble spot was Birmingham, Alabama, where Bull Connor repeatedly had the manager of the Greyhound station arrested for integrating the station's lunch counter. Not until January 1962 did a federal court order force Connor to stop prohibiting integration.

That same month, President John F. Kennedy said at a press conference that he viewed the integration of bus stations as one of the three important civil rights achievements of his presidency. He did not mention the role of the Freedom Riders in securing that victory.

The civil rights groups that had taken part in the Freedom Rides moved on to other projects. SNCC shifted its attention to voter registration. Starting late in 1961, the group focused its work in Georgia, Alabama, and Mississippi.

A long line of African-Americans waited outside an Alabama polling place to exercise their right to vote.

SNCC also joined with other groups in mass marches and other civil rights activities. James Bevel, one of the organizers of the second wave of Freedom Rides, helped direct a spring 1963 campaign aimed at desegregating stores in downtown Birmingham, Alabama. That effort succeeded despite the opposition of Bull Connor and his brutal use of attack dogs and fire hoses to punish protesters.

In the summer of 1963, SNCC helped organize the March on Washington. This massive, peaceful protest saw about 250,000 marchers walk toward the Lincoln Memorial to show their support for a civil rights law. Martin Luther King Jr. gave his famous "I Have a Dream" speech at this march. Freedom Rider John Lewis, then chairman of SNCC, also delivered an important address. In it, Lewis sharply criticized the major U.S. political parties for doing little to advance equal rights. He told the crowd that African-Americans should not wait for the rights they had long been denied:

> *To those who say 'be patient and wait,' we must say that we cannot be patient. We do not want our freedom gradually, but we want to be free now. We are tired. We are tired of being beaten by policemen. We are tired of seeing our people being locked up in jail over and over again. ... How long can we be patient? We want our freedom and we want it now. We do not want to go to jail, but we will go to jail if this is the price we must pay for love, brotherhood, and true peace.*

The March on Washington and other protests brought much attention to the civil rights movement. Eventually, President Lyndon Johnson, who became president when Kennedy was assassinated, convinced Congress to pass the Civil Rights Act of 1964. This breakthrough law banned discrimination in employment, housing, education, and many other areas. The federal government began forcing state governments in the South to take action to end segregation in many aspects of public life.

Television cameras showed President Lyndon B. Johnson reaching for a pen to sign the historic Civil Rights Act of 1964 into law.

81

In the summer of 1964, CORE launched a major voter-registration effort in Mississippi called Freedom Summer. SNCC workers joined with CORE to take part in Freedom Summer.

Hundreds of volunteers trained in the North and then fanned out through Mississippi. They taught African-Americans how to register to vote. They also taught reading and writing to those who had never received schooling and needed these skills so they could vote. Another part of the Freedom Summer project involved setting up Freedom Schools for young African-American children. Though marred by some violence, the campaign was successful. Tens of thousands of African-Americans in the South registered to vote.

THE MARTYRS OF FREEDOM SUMMER

The campaign known as Freedom Summer produced several casualties, and dozens of workers were beaten. Three civil rights workers—James Chaney, Andrew Goodman, and Michael Schwerner— were murdered. They had been arrested on trumped-up charges and disappeared, only to be found dead six weeks later. In December, the FBI arrested 21 white Southerners, including a deputy sheriff. Mississippi dropped charges against them, but they were later convicted in federal court for violating the workers' civil rights.

In 1965, SNCC led a voter-registration drive in Alabama. When state authorities blocked the effort, SNCC and the SCLC joined to stage a massive march from Selma to Montgomery, the state capital. On March 7, as John Lewis led 600 marchers across a bridge leaving Selma, they were met by Alabama state troopers, who brutally beat them with nightsticks and shot tear gas at them.

National outrage at the beating of the marchers helped spur Congress to do more to guarantee civil rights. President Johnson introduced a bill aimed at taking down all the obstacles that Southern states had erected to block African-Americans from voting. By early August, Congress had passed the bill and Johnson signed it into law. Once again, the federal government had stepped in to help put an end to the unfair treatment of black citizens.

The year 2001 marked the 40th anniversary of the Freedom Rides. Many riders joined in a celebration organized by Lewis. It included five people who had taken part in the first CORE Freedom Ride, which left Washington, D.C., in May 1961, and two veterans of the 1947 Journey of Reconciliation. Also in 2001, President Bill Clinton awarded the Presidential Citizens Medal to many veterans of the civil rights movement.

One of them was Irene Morgan Kirkaldy, then 84 years old. She was the woman who back in the 1940s had refused to leave her bus seat, an action that led to the 1946 Supreme Court decision integrating interstate buses. She—and the nation— had come a long way.

Thanks to laws such as the Civil Rights Act and the Voting Rights Act, African-Americans have made tremendous progress since the 1960s. Legal segregation has been dismantled in the South.

No longer do signs declare that certain restrooms or drinking fountains are for "whites only" or "colored only." Racial tension has subsided greatly across the South as well. The Ku Klux Klan and other hate groups have dwindled in membership and influence.

The power of the vote has made African-Americans a political force throughout the South. White Democrats such as Jimmy Carter and Bill Clinton won election as president in part because of their ability to win the votes of African-Americans in the South. Black politicians have enjoyed great success as well. John Lewis—veteran of the Freedom Rides—became a respected member of the U.S. House of Representatives and has served his district

In May 2006, John Lewis (center) and other members of Congress announced that they would reauthorize the Voting Rights Act for another 25 years.

in Georgia for more than 20 years. In 1990, Douglas Wilder of Virginia became the first African-American to be elected governor of any state.

African-Americans have enjoyed many advances since the 1950s and 1960s, but they still face some serious social and economic problems. While the Civil Rights Act afforded African-Americans, and all U.S. citizens, more opportunities and liberties, discrimination still exists in the United States in public education, at work, and even in the justice system. Freedom Riders and other civil rights activists played a pivotal role in ending segregation, but there is still a way to go before people of color are treated equally in the United States.

Nevertheless, the civil rights movement brought tremendous gains for African-Americans. These gains, which benefit everyone, are built on a foundation of bravery, sacrifice, and commitment. These advances were made possible by the vision and perseverance of the activists in the 1950s and 1960s who risked life and limb to challenge unfair laws. The gains are in part the result of the hard work and dedication of the people who took a chance and joined the Freedom Rides. ◣

Timeline

April 13, 1896
The U.S. Supreme Court rules in *Plessy v. Ferguson* that "separate but equal" facilities are constitutional.

May 30, 1909
The first conference of the National Association for the Advancement of Colored People (NAACP) begins.

1942
The Congress of Racial Equality (CORE) is founded.

June 3, 1946
The U.S. Supreme Court rules in *Morgan v. Virginia* that segregation on interstate buses is unconstitutional.

April 9–23, 1947
The Journey of Reconciliation is carried out by CORE.

July 26, 1948

President Harry S. Truman issues an executive order desegregating the armed forces.

December 5, 1955
Bus boycott begins in Montgomery, Alabama; it will last 381 days, when the city agrees to integrate the buses.

January 1957

Dr. Martin Luther King Jr. and others form the Southern Christian Leadership Conference (SCLC), a group dedicated to using nonviolent protest to end segregation.

February 1, 1960

Four students stage a lunch-counter sit-in in Greensboro, North Carolina; the sit-in movement later spreads to other cities.

April 16–18, 1960
African-American college students meet in Raleigh, North Carolina, and form the Student Nonviolent Coordinating Committee (SNCC).

December 5, 1960
The U.S. Supreme Court rules in *Boynton v. Virginia* that segregated interstate bus stations are unconstitutional.

May 4, 1961
The first wave of Freedom Riders, organized by CORE, leaves Washington, D.C.

May 13, 1961
The first wave of riders has dinner with King in Atlanta.

May 14, 1961

Attacks occur on the first wave of riders in Anniston and Birmingham, Alabama.

May 15, 1961
The first wave of riders flies from Birmingham, Alabama, to New Orleans, Louisiana.

May 17, 1961
The second wave of riders, organized by SNCC, travels from Nashville, Tennessee, to Birmingham; they are taken back to Tennessee by city police.

May 20, 1961
A larger group of riders travels under police escort from Birmingham to Montgomery, Alabama, where the riders are attacked.

May 21, 1961

A rally for riders at First Baptist Church in Montgomery is surrounded by a mob; the Alabama National Guard is called to the scene.

May 24, 1961
Two groups of riders travel from Montgomery, Alabama, to Jackson, Mississippi, largely under armed escort; the riders are arrested.

May 25, 1961
Seven Northerners and four African-American clergymen from the South are arrested in Montgomery before undertaking another Freedom Ride.

May 26, 1961

King and other civil rights leaders announce the formation of the Freedom Ride Coordinating Committee to continue the Freedom Rides during the summer.

May 29, 1961
Attorney General Robert F. Kennedy asks the Interstate Commerce Commission (ICC) to rule on segregated bus stations.

June 16, 1961
Attorney General Kennedy meets with civil rights activists to push voter registration as an alternative to Freedom Rides.

September 23, 1961
The ICC issues the ruling that segregated waiting rooms are illegal.

November 1, 1961
The ICC ruling takes effect.

Timeline

December 10, 1961
The last Freedom Ride takes place, a railroad journey by nine African-American and white riders from Atlanta to Albany, Georgia.

August 28, 1963
About 250,000 people join civil rights groups in the March on Washington.

June 20, 1964
The Freedom Summer voter-registration drive begins in Mississippi.

July 2, 1964

President Lyndon B. Johnson signs the Civil Rights Act of 1964 into law.

March 7, 1965
Civil rights demonstrators are beaten by Alabama state police outside Selma.

August 6, 1965
Johnson signs the Voting Rights Act of 1965 into law.

On the Web

For more information on this topic, use FactHound.

1 Go to *www.facthound.com*

2 Type in this book ID: 0756533333

3 Click on the *Fetch It!* button. FactHound will find the best Web sites for you.

Historic Sites

National Civil Rights Museum
450 Mulberry St.
Memphis, TN 38103
901/521-9699

The museum, converted from the motel where Martin Luther King Jr. was killed, contains exhibits on the key people and events of the civil rights movement.

Birmingham Civil Rights Institute
520 16th St. N.
Birmingham, AL 35203
205/328-9696

The museum has informational exhibits on the struggle for civil rights and stages events commemorating important steps in the movement.

Look For More Books in This Series

The Berlin Wall:
Barrier to Freedom

Black Tuesday:
Prelude to the Great Depression

A Day Without Immigrants:
Rallying Behind America's Newcomers

The March on Washington:
Uniting Against Racism

The National Grape Boycott:
A Victory for Farmworkers

The Teapot Dome Scandal:
Corruption Rocks 1920s America

Third Parties:
Influential Political Alternatives

A complete list of **Snapshots in History** titles is available on our Web site: *www.compasspointbooks.com*

Glossary

amendment
formal change made to a law or legal document, such as the Constitution

bail
fee paid to the criminal justice system to allow an accused person to be released from prison while awaiting trial

boycott
refuse to do business with someone as a form of protest

Constitution
document that describes the basic laws and principles by which the United States is governed

integration
opening up a place or organization to all, regardless of race

interstate
moving from one state to another

Interstate Commerce Commission
independent body of the federal government that has authority over the business-based movement of people and goods between states, including bus transportation

lynched
killed by a mob, usually by hanging

prejudice
negative feelings toward a particular group of people because of their race, religion, or ethnic background

segregation
practice of separating people of different races

seminary
school where students are trained to become ministers and priests

unconstitutional
law that goes against something set forth in the Constitution, the document that set up the government of the United States

voter registration
official process by which a citizen becomes eligible to vote; only registered voters can vote in an election

Source Notes

Chapter 1

Page 10, line 6: Raymond Arsenault. *Freedom Riders: 1961 and the Struggle for Racial Justice.* New York: Oxford University Press, 2006, p. 136.

Page 12, line 5: "IWFR: History of the Original Freedom Rides." Immigrant Workers Freedom Ride Coalition. 3 Sept 2006. www.iwfr.org/civilhistory.asp

Page 15, line 6: *Freedom Riders: 1961 and the Struggle for Racial Justice,* p. 160.

Chapter 2

Page 20, line 15: "*Plessy v. Ferguson (1896).*" Justia.com. 22 March 2007. www.supreme.justia.com/us/163/537/case.html

Page 23, line 6: William Loren Katz. *Eyewitness: A Living Documentary of the African-American Contribution to American History.* Rev. ed. New York: Touchstone, 1995, p. 334.

Page 23, line 19: Ibid., p. 335.

Chapter 3

Page 29, line 11: *Freedom Riders: 1961 and the Struggle for Racial Justice,* p. 52.

Page 35, line 4: Juan Williams. *Eyes on the Prize: America's Civil Rights Years, 1954–1965.* New York: Penguin Books, 1988, p. 133.

Page 36, line 23: Clayborne Carson. *In Struggle: SNCC and the Black Awakening of the 1960s.* Cambridge, Mass.: Harvard University Press, 1995, p. 23.

Chapter 4

Page 43, line 30: Taylor Branch. *Parting the Waters: America in the King Years, 1954–63.* New York: Touchstone, 1988, p. 417.

Page 44, line 6: James Farmer. *Lay Bare the Heart: An Autobiography of the Civil Rights Movement.* New York: Arbor House, 1985, p. 201.

Chapter 5

Page 49, line 4: Ibid., p. 430.

Page 53, line 29: *Parting the Waters: America in the King Years, 1954–63,* p. 443.

Page 57, line 7: *Freedom Riders: 1961 and the Struggle for Racial Justice,* p. 224.

Source Notes

Chapter 6

Page 69, sidebar, line 7: David Niven. *The Politics of Injustice: The Kennedys, the Freedom Rides, and the Electoral Consequences of a Moral Compromise.* Knoxville: University of Tennessee Press, 2003, p. 107.

Page 69, sidebar, line 10: *Parting the Waters: America in the King Years, 1954–63,* p. 474.

Chapter 7

Page 72, sidebar: *Freedom Riders: 1961 and the Struggle for Racial Justice,* p. 281.

Page 73, line 6: Peter B. Levy. *Let Freedom Ring: A Documentary History of the Modern Civil Rights Movement.* New York: Praeger, 1992, p. 80.

Page 74, line 5: *The Politics of Injustice: The Kennedys, the Freedom Rides, and the Electoral Consequences of a Moral Compromise,* p. 111.

Page 75, line 10: Ibid, p. 111.

Chapter 8

Page 80, line 22: Sanford Wexler. *The Civil Rights Movement: An Eyewitness History.* New York: Facts on File, 1993, p. 187.

SELECT BIBLIOGRAPHY

Arsenault, Raymond. *Freedom Riders: 1961 and the Struggle for Racial Justice.*
New York: Oxford University Press, 2006.

Branch, Taylor. *Parting the Waters: America in the King Years, 1954–63.*
New York: Touchstone, 1988.

Carson, Clayborne. *In Struggle: SNCC and the Black Awakening of the 1960s.*
Cambridge, Mass.: Harvard University Press, 1995.

Halberstam, David. *The Children.* New York: Random House, 1998.

Katz, William Loren. *Eyewitness: A Living Documentary of the African-American
Contribution to American History.* Rev. ed. New York: Touchstone, 1995.

Levy, Peter B. *Let Freedom Ring: A Documentary History of the Modern Civil
Rights Movement.* New York: Praeger, 1992.

Niven, David. *The Politics of Injustice: The Kennedys, the Freedom Rides,
and the Electoral Consequences of a Moral Compromise.* Knoxville: University
of Tennessee Press, 2003.

Williams, Juan. *Eyes on the Prize: America's Civil Rights Years, 1954–1965.*
New York: Penguin, 1987.

FURTHER READING

Haskins, James. *Freedom Rides: Journey for Justice.* New York:
Hyperion Books for Children, 1995.

Hill, Cristine M. *John Lewis: From Freedom Rider to Congressman.*
Springfield, N.J.: Enslow, 2002.

McWhorter, Diane. *A Dream of Freedom: The Civil Rights Movement from
1954 to 1968.* New York: Scholastic, 2004.

Levine, Ellen. *Freedom's Children: Young Civil Rights Activisits Tell their Own Stories.*
New York: Putnam, 2000.

Olson, Lynne. *Freedom's Daughters: The Unsung Heroines of the Civil Rights
Movement from 1830 to 1970.* New York: Scribner's, 2001.

Sirimarco, Elizabeth. *The Civil Rights Movement.* New York:
Benchmark Books, 2005.

Index

ABOUT THE AUTHOR

Dale Anderson studied history and literature at Harvard College. He has worked in publishing ever since. He now lives with his wife and two sons in Newtown, Pennsylvania, where he writes and edits textbooks and library books. He has written several books for young adults, including books on the Tet Offensive, the Watergate scandal, and the Republican Party in the Snapshots series.

IMAGE CREDITS